before amen

PRAYER JOURNAL

MAX LUCADO

THOMAS NELSON
Since 1798

NASHVILLE   MEXICO CITY   RIO DE JANEIRO

Published in Nashville, Tennessee, by Thomas Nelson, a division of HarperCollins Christian Publishing, Inc.

Thomas Nelson titles may be purchased in bulk for educational, business, fund-raising, or sales promotional use. For information, please e-mail *SpecialMarkets@ThomasNelson.com*.

Unless otherwise noted, Scripture quotations are taken from the New King James Version®. © 1982 by Thomas Nelson, Inc. Used by permission. All rights reserved.

Other Scripture references are from the following sources: NEW AMERICAN STANDARD BIBLE® (NASB). © The Lockman Foundation 1960, 1962, 1963, 1968, 1971, 1972, 1973, 1975, 1977, 1995. Used by permission. New Century Version® (NCV). © 2005 by Thomas Nelson, Inc. Used by permission. Holy Bible, New International Version®, NIV® (NIV). © 1973, 1978, 1984, 2011 by Biblica, Inc.™ Used by permission of Zondervan. All rights reserved worldwide. www.zondervan.com. *Holy Bible*, New Living Translation (NLT). © 1996, 2004, 2007. Used by permission of Tyndale House Publishers, Inc., Wheaton, Illinois 60189. All rights reserved.

ISBN 978-0-7180-1406-3

Printed in China

14 15 16 17 18 RRD 5 4 3 2 1

www.thomasnelson.com

An Introduction to the Pocket Prayer

Hello, my name is Max. I'm a recovering prayer wimp. I doze off when I pray. My thoughts zig, then zag, then zig again. Distractions swarm like gnats on a summer night. If attention deficit disorder applies to prayer, I am afflicted. When I pray, I think of a thousand things I need to do. I forget the one thing I set out to do: pray.

Some people excel in prayer. They inhale heaven and exhale God. They are the SEAL Team Six of intercession. They would rather pray than sleep. Why is it that I sleep when I pray? They belong to the PGA: Prayer Giants Association. I am a card-carrying member of the PWA: Prayer Wimps Anonymous.

Can you relate? It's not that we don't pray at all. We all pray some.

On tearstained pillows we pray.

In grand liturgies we pray.

At the sight of geese in flight, we pray.

Quoting ancient devotions, we pray.

We pray to stay sober, centered, or solvent. We pray when the lump is deemed malignant. When the money runs out before the month does. When the unborn baby hasn't kicked in a while. We all pray . . . some.

But wouldn't we all like to pray . . .

More?

Better?

Deeper?

Stronger?

With more fire, faith, or fervency?

Yet we have kids to feed, bills to pay, deadlines to meet. The calendar pounces on our good intentions like a tiger on a rabbit. We want to pray, but *when*?

We want to pray, but *why*? We might as well admit it. Prayer is odd, peculiar. Speaking into space. Lifting words into the sky. We can't even get the cable company to answer us, yet God will? The doctor is too busy, but God isn't? We have our doubts about prayer.

And we have our checkered history with prayer: unmet expectations, unanswered requests. We can barely genuflect for the scar tissue on our knees. God, to some, is the ultimate heartbreaker. Why keep tossing the coins of our longings into a silent pool? He jilted me once . . . but not twice.

Oh, the peculiar puzzle of prayer.

We aren't the first to struggle. The sign-up sheet for Prayer 101 contains some familiar names: the apostles John, James, Andrew, and Peter. When one of Jesus' disciples requested, "Lord, teach us to pray" (Luke 11:1 NIV), none of the others objected. No one walked away saying, "Hey, I have prayer figured out." The first followers of Jesus needed prayer guidance.

In fact, the only tutorial they ever requested was on prayer. They could have asked for instructions on many topics: bread multiplying, speech making, storm stilling. Jesus raised people from the dead. But a "How to Vacate the Cemetery" seminar? His followers never called for one. But they did want him to do this: "Lord, teach us to pray."

Might their interest have had something to do with the jaw-dropping, eye-popping promises Jesus attached to prayer? "Ask and it will be given to you" (Matt. 7:7 NIV). "If you believe, you will get anything you ask for in prayer" (Matt. 21:22 NCV). Jesus never attached such power to other endeavors. "*Plan* and it will be given to you." "You will get anything you *work* for." Those words are not in the Bible. But these are— "If you remain in me and follow my teachings, you can ask anything you want, and it will be given to you" (John 15:7 NCV).

Jesus gave stunning prayer promises.

And he set a compelling prayer example. Jesus prayed before he ate. He prayed for children. He prayed for the sick. He prayed with thanks. He prayed with tears. He had made the planets and shaped the stars, yet he prayed. He is the Lord of angels and Commander of heavenly hosts, yet he prayed. He is coequal with God, the exact representation of the Holy One, and yet he devoted himself to prayer. He prayed in the desert, cemetery, and garden. "He went out and departed to a solitary place; and there He prayed" (Mark 1:35).

This dialogue must have been common among his friends:

"Has anyone seen Jesus?"

"Oh, you know. He's up to the same thing."

"Praying *again*?

"Yep. He's been gone since sunrise."

Jesus would even disappear for an entire night of prayer. I'm thinking of one occasion in particular. He'd just experienced one of the most stressful days of his ministry. The day began with the news of the death of his relative John the Baptist. Jesus sought to retreat with his disciples, yet a throng of thousands followed him. Though grief-stricken, he spent the day teaching and healing people. When it was discovered that the host of people had no food to eat, Jesus multiplied bread out of a basket and fed the entire multitude. In the span of a few hours, he battled sorrow, stress, demands, and needs. He deserved a good night's rest. Yet when evening finally came, he told the crowd to leave and the disciples to board their boat, and "he went up into the hills by himself to pray" (Mark 6:46 NLT).

Apparently it was the correct choice. A storm exploded over the Sea of Galilee, leaving the disciples "in trouble far away from land, for a strong wind had risen, and they were fighting heavy waves. About three o'clock in the morning Jesus came toward them, walking on the water" (Matt. 14:24–25 NLT). Jesus ascended the mountain depleted. He reappeared invigorated. When he reached the water, he never broke his stride. You'd have thought the water was a park lawn and the storm a spring breeze.

Do you think the disciples made the prayer–power connection? "Lord, teach us to pray *like that*. Teach us to find strength in prayer. To banish fear in prayer. To defy storms in prayer. To come off the mountain of prayer with the authority of a prince."

What about you? The disciples faced angry waves and a watery grave. You face angry clients, a turbulent economy, raging seas of stress and sorrow.

"Lord," we still request, "teach us to pray."

When the disciples asked Jesus to teach them to pray,

he gave them a prayer. Not a lecture on prayer. Not the doctrine of prayer. He gave them a quotable, repeatable, portable prayer (Luke 11:1–4).

Could you use the same? It seems to me that the prayers of the Bible can be distilled into one. The result is a simple, easy-to-remember, pocket-size prayer:

> *Father,*
>> *you are good.*
>>> *I need help. Heal me and forgive me.*
>>> *They need help.*
>>> *Thank you.*
>>> *In Jesus' name, amen.*

Let this prayer punctuate your day. As you begin your morning, *Father, you are good.* As you commute to work or walk the hallways at school, *I need help.* As you wait in the grocery line, *They need help.* Keep this prayer in your pocket as you pass through the day.

When we invite God into our world, he walks in. He brings a host of gifts: joy, patience, resilience. Anxieties come, but they don't stick. Fears surface and then depart. Regrets land on the windshield, but then comes the wiper of prayer. The devil still hands me stones of guilt, but I turn and give them to Christ. I'm completing my sixth decade, yet I'm wired with energy. I am happier, healthier, and more hopeful than I have ever been. Struggles come, for sure. But so does God.

Prayer is not a privilege for the pious, not the art of a chosen few. Prayer is simply a heartfelt conversation between God and his child. My friend, he wants to talk with you. Even now, as you read these words, he taps at the door. Open it. Welcome him in. Let the conversation begin.

> *Prayer is simply a heartfelt conversation between God and his child.*

Father,
You are good.

_____

_____

_____

_____

_____

_____

_____

I need help.

_____

_____

_____

_____

_____

_____

_____

They need help.

_____

_____

_____

_____

_____

_____

_____

_____

_____

Thank you.

_____

_____

_____

_____

_____

_____

_____

_____

_____

In Jesus' name, amen.

> *We speak. He listens. He speaks.*
> *We listen. This is prayer in its*
> *purest form. God changes his*
> *people through such moments.*

Father,

You are good.

_____

_____

_____

_____

_____

_____

_____

I need help.

_____

_____

_____

_____

_____

_____

_____

They need help.

_____

_____

_____

_____

_____

_____

_____

_____

_____

Thank you.

_____

_____

_____

_____

_____

_____

_____

_____

_____

In Jesus' name, amen.

> *Prayer begins with an honest,*
> *heartfelt "Oh, Daddy."*

Father,

You are good.

_____

_____

_____

_____

_____

_____

_____

I need help.

_____

_____

_____

_____

_____

_____

_____

They need help.

_____

_____

_____

_____

_____

_____

_____

_____

_____

Thank you.

_____

_____

_____

_____

_____

_____

_____

_____

In Jesus' name, amen.

*Jesus invites us to approach
God the way a child approaches
his or her daddy.*

Father,
You are good.

_____

_____

_____

_____

_____

_____

_____

I need help.

_____

_____

_____

_____

_____

_____

_____

They need help.

_____

_____

_____

_____

_____

_____

_____

_____

_____

Thank you.

_____

_____

_____

_____

_____

_____

_____

_____

_____

In Jesus' name, amen.

> *If God is at once Father and Creator, holy—unlike us—and high above us, then we at any point are only a prayer away from help.*

Father,
You are good.

_____

_____

_____

_____

_____

_____

_____

I need help.

_____

_____

_____

_____

_____

_____

_____

_____

They need help.

_____

_____

_____

_____

_____

_____

_____

_____

Thank you.

_____

_____

_____

_____

_____

_____

_____

_____

In Jesus' name, amen.

> *Before you face the world,*
> *face your Father.*

Father,

You are good.

_____

_____

_____

_____

_____

_____

_____

I need help.

_____

_____

_____

_____

_____

_____

_____

They need help.

_____

_____

_____

_____

_____

_____

_____

_____

_____

Thank you.

_____

_____

_____

_____

_____

_____

_____

_____

In Jesus' name, amen.

> *"Be anxious for nothing, but in everything by prayer and supplication, with thanksgiving, let your requests be made known to God"* (Phil. 4:6).

Father,

You are good.

_____

_____

_____

_____

_____

_____

_____

I need help.

_____

_____

_____

_____

_____

_____

_____

They need help.

_____

_____

_____

_____

_____

_____

_____

_____

Thank you.

_____

_____

_____

_____

_____

_____

_____

_____

In Jesus' name, amen.

God keeps his word.
We just need to ask.

Father,
You are good.

_____

_____

_____

_____

_____

_____

_____

I need help.

_____

_____

_____

_____

_____

_____

_____

They need help.

_____

_____

_____

_____

_____

_____

_____

_____

_____

Thank you.

_____

_____

_____

_____

_____

_____

_____

_____

In Jesus' name, amen.

> *"Cast all your anxiety on him because he cares for you"* (1 Peter 5:7 *NIV*).

Father,

You are good.

_____

_____

_____

_____

_____

_____

_____

I need help.

_____

_____

_____

_____

_____

_____

_____

They need help.

Thank you.

In Jesus' name, amen.

> *Jesus never refused an*
> *intercessory request. Ever!*

Father,
You are good.

_____

_____

_____

_____

_____

_____

_____

I need help.

_____

_____

_____

_____

_____

_____

_____

_____

They need help.

_____

_____

_____

_____

_____

_____

_____

_____

Thank you.

_____

_____

_____

_____

_____

_____

_____

_____

In Jesus' name, amen.

"[God] is able to do exceedingly abundantly above all that we ask or think" (Eph. 3:20).

Father,
You are good.

_____

_____

_____

_____

_____

_____

_____

I need help.

_____

_____

_____

_____

_____

_____

_____

They need help.

_____

_____

_____

_____

_____

_____

_____

_____

_____

Thank you.

_____

_____

_____

_____

_____

_____

_____

_____

_____

In Jesus' name, amen.

> *Nothing pleases Jesus as much
> as being audaciously trusted.*

Father,

You are good.

_____

_____

_____

_____

_____

_____

_____

I need help.

_____

_____

_____

_____

_____

_____

_____

They need help.

_____

_____

_____

_____

_____

_____

_____

_____

Thank you.

_____

_____

_____

_____

_____

_____

_____

_____

In Jesus' name, amen.

> *"God will supply all [our] needs according to His riches" (Phil. 4:19 NASB).*

Father,

You are good.

_____

_____

_____

_____

_____

_____

_____

I need help.

_____

_____

_____

_____

_____

_____

_____

They need help.

_____

_____

_____

_____

_____

_____

_____

_____

_____

Thank you.

_____

_____

_____

_____

_____

_____

_____

_____

_____

In Jesus' name, amen.

> *You are never more like Jesus*
> *than when you pray for others.*

Father,
You are good.

_____

_____

_____

_____

_____

_____

_____

I need help.

_____

_____

_____

_____

_____

_____

_____

They need help.

_____

_____

_____

_____

_____

_____

_____

_____

_____

Thank you.

_____

_____

_____

_____

_____

_____

_____

_____

_____

In Jesus' name, amen.

> *"Truly, truly, I say to you, if you ask the Father for anything in My name, He will give it to you"* (John 16:23 NASB).

Father,

You are good.

_____

_____

_____

_____

_____

_____

_____

I need help.

_____

_____

_____

_____

_____

_____

_____

They need help.

_____

_____

_____

_____

_____

_____

_____

_____

_____

Thank you.

_____

_____

_____

_____

_____

_____

_____

_____

In Jesus' name, amen.

> *Prayer is not a magical
> formula or a mystical chant.
> It is the yes to God's invitation
> to invoke his name.*

Father,
You are good.

_____
_____
_____
_____
_____
_____
_____

I need help.

_____
_____
_____
_____
_____
_____
_____

They need help.

_____

_____

_____

_____

_____

_____

_____

_____

_____

Thank you.

_____

_____

_____

_____

_____

_____

_____

_____

_____

In Jesus' name, amen.

> *Since God works, prayer works.*
> *Since God is good, prayer is good.*
> *Since you matter to God, your*
> *prayers matter in heaven.*

Father,
You are good.

_____

_____

_____

_____

_____

_____

_____

I need help.

_____

_____

_____

_____

_____

_____

_____

_____

They need help.

_____

_____

_____

_____

_____

_____

_____

_____

_____

Thank you.

_____

_____

_____

_____

_____

_____

_____

_____

_____

In Jesus' name, amen.

*You're never without hope, because
you're never without prayer.*

Father,
You are good.

I need help.

They need help.

_____

_____

_____

_____

_____

_____

_____

_____

_____

Thank you.

_____

_____

_____

_____

_____

_____

_____

_____

_____

In Jesus' name, amen.

Father,
You are good.

_____

_____

_____

_____

_____

_____

_____

I need help.

_____

_____

_____

_____

_____

_____

_____

They need help.

_____

_____

_____

_____

_____

_____

_____

_____

_____

_____

Thank you.

_____

_____

_____

_____

_____

_____

_____

_____

_____

_____

In Jesus' name, amen.

> *We speak. He listens. He speaks.*
> *We listen. This is prayer in its*
> *purest form. God changes his*
> *people through such moments.*

Father,
You are good.

_____

_____

_____

_____

_____

_____

_____

I need help.

_____

_____

_____

_____

_____

_____

_____

They need help.

_____

_____

_____

_____

_____

_____

_____

_____

Thank you.

_____

_____

_____

_____

_____

_____

_____

_____

In Jesus' name, amen.

> *Prayer begins with an honest,*
> *heartfelt "Oh, Daddy."*

Father,
You are good.

_____

_____

_____

_____

_____

_____

_____

I need help.

_____

_____

_____

_____

_____

_____

_____

_____

They need help.

_____

_____

_____

_____

_____

_____

_____

_____

Thank you.

_____

_____

_____

_____

_____

_____

_____

In Jesus' name, amen.

*Jesus invites us to approach
God the way a child approaches
his or her daddy.*

Father,
You are good.

_____

_____

_____

_____

_____

_____

_____

I need help.

_____

_____

_____

_____

_____

_____

_____

They need help.

_____

_____

_____

_____

_____

_____

_____

_____

Thank you.

_____

_____

_____

_____

_____

_____

_____

_____

In Jesus' name, amen.

> *If God is at once Father and Creator, holy—unlike us—and high above us, then we at any point are only a prayer away from help.*

Father,
You are good.

_____

_____

_____

_____

_____

_____

_____

I need help.

_____

_____

_____

_____

_____

_____

_____

_____

They need help.

_____

_____

_____

_____

_____

_____

_____

_____

_____

Thank you.

_____

_____

_____

_____

_____

_____

_____

_____

_____

In Jesus' name, amen.

Before you face the world,
face your Father.

Father,
You are good.

_____

_____

_____

_____

_____

_____

_____

I need help.

_____

_____

_____

_____

_____

_____

_____

They need help.

_____

_____

_____

_____

_____

_____

_____

_____

_____

Thank you.

_____

_____

_____

_____

_____

_____

_____

_____

In Jesus' name, amen.

> *"Be anxious for nothing, but in everything by prayer and supplication, with thanksgiving, let your requests be made known to God"* (Phil. 4:6).

Father,
You are good.

_____

_____

_____

_____

_____

_____

_____

I need help.

_____

_____

_____

_____

_____

_____

_____

_____

They need help.

_____

_____

_____

_____

_____

_____

_____

_____

_____

_____

Thank you.

_____

_____

_____

_____

_____

_____

_____

_____

_____

_____

In Jesus' name, amen.

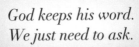

God keeps his word.
We just need to ask.

Father,
You are good.

_____

_____

_____

_____

_____

_____

_____

I need help.

_____

_____

_____

_____

_____

_____

_____

_____

They need help.

_____

_____

_____

_____

_____

_____

_____

_____

_____

Thank you.

_____

_____

_____

_____

_____

_____

_____

_____

_____

In Jesus' name, amen.

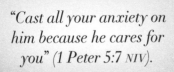

"Cast all your anxiety on him because he cares for you" (1 Peter 5:7 *NIV*).

Father,
You are good.

_____

_____

_____

_____

_____

_____

_____

_____

I need help.

_____

_____

_____

_____

_____

_____

_____

_____

_____

They need help.

_____

_____

_____

_____

_____

_____

_____

_____

Thank you.

_____

_____

_____

_____

_____

_____

_____

_____

In Jesus' name, amen.

> *Jesus never refused an intercessory request. Ever!*

Father,

You are good.

_____

_____

_____

_____

_____

_____

_____

I need help.

_____

_____

_____

_____

_____

_____

_____

They need help.

_____

_____

_____

_____

_____

_____

_____

_____

Thank you.

_____

_____

_____

_____

_____

_____

_____

_____

In Jesus' name, amen.

> "[God] is able to do exceedingly
> abundantly above all that we
> ask or think" (Eph. 3:20).

Father,
You are good.

_____

_____

_____

_____

_____

_____

_____

I need help.

_____

_____

_____

_____

_____

_____

_____

They need help.

_____

_____

_____

_____

_____

_____

_____

_____

Thank you.

_____

_____

_____

_____

_____

_____

_____

_____

In Jesus' name, amen.

*Nothing pleases Jesus as much
as being audaciously trusted.*

Father,
You are good.

_____

_____

_____

_____

_____

_____

_____

I need help.

_____

_____

_____

_____

_____

_____

_____

They need help.

_____

_____

_____

_____

_____

_____

_____

_____

Thank you.

_____

_____

_____

_____

_____

_____

_____

_____

In Jesus' name, amen.

> *"God will supply all [our] needs according to His riches" (Phil. 4:19 NASB).*

Father,

You are good.

_____

_____

_____

_____

_____

_____

_____

I need help.

_____

_____

_____

_____

_____

_____

_____

They need help.

_____

_____

_____

_____

_____

_____

_____

_____

Thank you.

_____

_____

_____

_____

_____

_____

_____

In Jesus' name, amen.

> *You are never more like Jesus*
> *than when you pray for others.*

Father,
You are good.

_____

_____

_____

_____

_____

_____

_____

I need help.

_____

_____

_____

_____

_____

_____

_____

They need help.

_____

_____

_____

_____

_____

_____

_____

_____

Thank you.

_____

_____

_____

_____

_____

_____

_____

_____

In Jesus' name, amen.

Father,

You are good.

_____

_____

_____

_____

_____

_____

_____

I need help.

_____

_____

_____

_____

_____

_____

_____

_____

They need help.

_____

_____

_____

_____

_____

_____

_____

_____

Thank you.

_____

_____

_____

_____

_____

_____

_____

_____

In Jesus' name, amen.

*Prayer is not a magical
formula or a mystical chant.
It is the yes to God's invitation
to invoke his name.*

Father,
You are good.

_____

_____

_____

_____

_____

_____

_____

_____

I need help.

_____

_____

_____

_____

_____

_____

_____

_____

They need help.

_____

_____

_____

_____

_____

_____

_____

_____

_____

Thank you.

_____

_____

_____

_____

_____

_____

_____

_____

_____

In Jesus' name, amen.

Father,
You are good.

_____

_____

_____

_____

_____

_____

_____

I need help.

_____

_____

_____

_____

_____

_____

_____

They need help.

_____

_____

_____

_____

_____

_____

_____

_____

_____

Thank you.

_____

_____

_____

_____

_____

_____

_____

_____

_____

In Jesus' name, amen.

> *You're never without hope, because*
> *you're never without prayer.*

Father,
You are good.

_____

_____

_____

_____

_____

_____

_____

I need help.

_____

_____

_____

_____

_____

_____

_____

They need help.

_____

_____

_____

_____

_____

_____

_____

_____

_____

Thank you.

_____

_____

_____

_____

_____

_____

_____

_____

_____

In Jesus' name, amen.

*Prayer is simply a heartfelt
conversation between
God and his child.*

Father,
You are good.

_____

_____

_____

_____

_____

_____

_____

I need help.

_____

_____

_____

_____

_____

_____

_____

They need help.

_____

_____

_____

_____

_____

_____

_____

_____

Thank you.

_____

_____

_____

_____

_____

_____

_____

_____

In Jesus' name, amen.

> *We speak. He listens. He speaks.*
> *We listen. This is prayer in its*
> *purest form. God changes his*
> *people through such moments.*

Father,
You are good.

_____

_____

_____

_____

_____

_____

_____

I need help.

_____

_____

_____

_____

_____

_____

_____

They need help.

_____

_____

_____

_____

_____

_____

_____

_____

_____

Thank you.

_____

_____

_____

_____

_____

_____

_____

_____

_____

In Jesus' name, amen.

Father,
You are good.

_____

_____

_____

_____

_____

_____

_____

_____

I need help.

_____

_____

_____

_____

_____

_____

_____

_____

They need help.

_____

_____

_____

_____

_____

_____

_____

_____

_____

Thank you.

_____

_____

_____

_____

_____

_____

_____

_____

_____

In Jesus' name, amen.

*Jesus invites us to approach
God the way a child approaches
his or her daddy.*

Father,
You are good.

_____

_____

_____

_____

_____

_____

_____

I need help.

_____

_____

_____

_____

_____

_____

_____

_____

They need help.

_____

_____

_____

_____

_____

_____

_____

_____

_____

Thank you.

_____

_____

_____

_____

_____

_____

_____

_____

In Jesus' name, amen.

> *If God is at once Father and Creator, holy—unlike us—and high above us, then we at any point are only a prayer away from help.*

Father,
You are good.

_____

_____

_____

_____

_____

_____

_____

I need help.

_____

_____

_____

_____

_____

_____

_____

_____

They need help.

_____

_____

_____

_____

_____

_____

_____

_____

_____

Thank you.

_____

_____

_____

_____

_____

_____

_____

_____

_____

In Jesus' name, amen.

> *Before you face the world,*
> *face your Father.*

Father,
You are good.

_____

_____

_____

_____

_____

_____

_____

I need help.

_____

_____

_____

_____

_____

_____

_____

They need help.

_____

_____

_____

_____

_____

_____

_____

_____

_____

Thank you.

_____

_____

_____

_____

_____

_____

_____

_____

In Jesus' name, amen.

> *"Be anxious for nothing, but in everything by prayer and supplication, with thanksgiving, let your requests be made known to God"* (Phil. 4:6).

Father,
You are good.

_____

_____

_____

_____

_____

_____

_____

I need help.

_____

_____

_____

_____

_____

_____

_____

They need help.

_____

_____

_____

_____

_____

_____

_____

_____

_____

Thank you.

_____

_____

_____

_____

_____

_____

_____

_____

In Jesus' name, amen.

> *God keeps his word.*
> *We just need to ask.*

Father,
You are good.

_____

_____

_____

_____

_____

_____

_____

I need help.

_____

_____

_____

_____

_____

_____

_____

They need help.

_____

_____

_____

_____

_____

_____

_____

_____

Thank you.

_____

_____

_____

_____

_____

_____

_____

_____

In Jesus' name, amen.

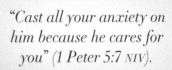

Father,
You are good.

_____

_____

_____

_____

_____

_____

_____

I need help.

_____

_____

_____

_____

_____

_____

_____

They need help.

Thank you.

In Jesus' name, amen.

*Jesus never refused an
intercessory request. Ever!*

Father,

You are good.

I need help.

They need help.

_____

_____

_____

_____

_____

_____

_____

_____

Thank you.

_____

_____

_____

_____

_____

_____

_____

_____

In Jesus' name, amen.

*"[God] is able to do exceedingly
abundantly above all that we
ask or think" (Eph. 3:20).*

Father,

You are good.

_____

_____

_____

_____

_____

_____

_____

_____

I need help.

_____

_____

_____

_____

_____

_____

_____

They need help.

_____

_____

_____

_____

_____

_____

_____

_____

_____

Thank you.

_____

_____

_____

_____

_____

_____

_____

_____

_____

In Jesus' name, amen.

> *Nothing pleases Jesus as much
> as being audaciously trusted.*

Father,

You are good.

_____

_____

_____

_____

_____

_____

_____

I need help.

_____

_____

_____

_____

_____

_____

_____

They need help.

_____

_____

_____

_____

_____

_____

_____

_____

Thank you.

_____

_____

_____

_____

_____

_____

_____

_____

In Jesus' name, amen.

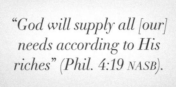

"God will supply all [our] needs according to His riches" (Phil. 4:19 NASB).

Father,
You are good.

_____

_____

_____

_____

_____

_____

_____

_____

I need help.

_____

_____

_____

_____

_____

_____

_____

_____

They need help.

_____

_____

_____

_____

_____

_____

_____

_____

Thank you.

_____

_____

_____

_____

_____

_____

_____

_____

In Jesus' name, amen.

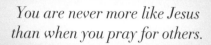

*You are never more like Jesus
than when you pray for others.*

Father,
You are good.

_____

_____

_____

_____

_____

_____

_____

I need help.

_____

_____

_____

_____

_____

_____

_____

They need help.

_____

_____

_____

_____

_____

_____

_____

_____

Thank you.

_____

_____

_____

_____

_____

_____

_____

_____

In Jesus' name, amen.

> *"Truly, truly, I say to you, if you ask the Father for anything in My name, He will give it to you"* (John 16:23 *NASB*).

Father,
You are good.

_____

_____

_____

_____

_____

_____

_____

I need help.

_____

_____

_____

_____

_____

_____

_____

They need help.

_____

_____

_____

_____

_____

_____

_____

_____

Thank you.

_____

_____

_____

_____

_____

_____

_____

_____

In Jesus' name, amen.

*Prayer is not a magical
formula or a mystical chant.
It is the yes to God's invitation
to invoke his name.*

Father,
You are good.

_____

_____

_____

_____

_____

_____

_____

I need help.

_____

_____

_____

_____

_____

_____

_____

They need help.

_____

_____

_____

_____

_____

_____

_____

_____

Thank you.

_____

_____

_____

_____

_____

_____

_____

In Jesus' name, amen.

Since God works, prayer works.
Since God is good, prayer is good.
Since you matter to God, your
prayers matter in heaven.

Father,
You are good.

_____

_____

_____

_____

_____

_____

_____

I need help.

_____

_____

_____

_____

_____

_____

_____

They need help.

Thank you.

In Jesus' name, amen.

> *You're never without hope, because you're never without prayer.*

Father,
You are good.

_____

_____

_____

_____

_____

_____

_____

I need help.

_____

_____

_____

_____

_____

_____

_____

They need help.

_____

_____

_____

_____

_____

_____

_____

_____

_____

Thank you.

_____

_____

_____

_____

_____

_____

_____

_____

_____

In Jesus' name, amen.

> *Prayer is simply a heartfelt conversation between God and his child.*

Father,
You are good.

_____

_____

_____

_____

_____

_____

_____

I need help.

_____

_____

_____

_____

_____

_____

_____

They need help.

_____

_____

_____

_____

_____

_____

_____

_____

Thank you.

_____

_____

_____

_____

_____

_____

_____

_____

In Jesus' name, amen.

> *We speak. He listens. He speaks.*
> *We listen. This is prayer in its*
> *purest form. God changes his*
> *people through such moments.*

Father,
You are good.

_____

_____

_____

_____

_____

_____

_____

I need help.

_____

_____

_____

_____

_____

_____

_____

They need help.

Thank you.

In Jesus' name, amen.

> *Prayer begins with an honest,*
> *heartfelt "Oh, Daddy."*

Father,
You are good.

_____

_____

_____

_____

_____

_____

_____

I need help.

_____

_____

_____

_____

_____

_____

_____

_____

They need help.

_____

_____

_____

_____

_____

_____

_____

_____

Thank you.

_____

_____

_____

_____

_____

_____

_____

_____

In Jesus' name, amen.

> *Jesus invites us to approach God the way a child approaches his or her daddy.*

Father,
You are good.

_____

_____

_____

_____

_____

_____

_____

I need help.

_____

_____

_____

_____

_____

_____

_____

They need help.

_____

_____

_____

_____

_____

_____

_____

_____

_____

Thank you.

_____

_____

_____

_____

_____

_____

_____

_____

In Jesus' name, amen.

> *If God is at once Father and Creator, holy—unlike us—and high above us, then we at any point are only a prayer away from help.*

Father,
You are good.

_____

_____

_____

_____

_____

_____

_____

I need help.

_____

_____

_____

_____

_____

_____

_____

_____

They need help.

_____

_____

_____

_____

_____

_____

_____

_____

Thank you.

_____

_____

_____

_____

_____

_____

_____

_____

In Jesus' name, amen.

> *Before you face the world,*
> *face your Father.*

Father,
You are good.

_____

_____

_____

_____

_____

_____

_____

I need help.

_____

_____

_____

_____

_____

_____

_____

They need help.

_____

_____

_____

_____

_____

_____

_____

_____

Thank you.

_____

_____

_____

_____

_____

_____

_____

_____

In Jesus' name, amen.

> *"Be anxious for nothing, but in everything by prayer and supplication, with thanksgiving, let your requests be made known to God"* (Phil. 4:6).

Father,

You are good.

I need help.

They need help.

_____

_____

_____

_____

_____

_____

_____

_____

Thank you.

_____

_____

_____

_____

_____

_____

_____

_____

In Jesus' name, amen.

> *God keeps his word.*
> *We just need to ask.*

Father,
You are good.

_____

_____

_____

_____

_____

_____

_____

I need help.

_____

_____

_____

_____

_____

_____

_____

They need help.

Thank you.

In Jesus' name, amen.

> *"Cast all your anxiety on him because he cares for you"* (1 Peter 5:7 *NIV*).

Father,
You are good.

_____

_____

_____

_____

_____

_____

_____

I need help.

_____

_____

_____

_____

_____

_____

_____

They need help.

_____

_____

_____

_____

_____

_____

_____

_____

_____

Thank you.

_____

_____

_____

_____

_____

_____

_____

_____

_____

In Jesus' name, amen.

> *Jesus never refused an*
> *intercessory request. Ever!*

Father,
You are good.

_____

_____

_____

_____

_____

_____

_____

I need help.

_____

_____

_____

_____

_____

_____

_____

_____

They need help.

Thank you.

In Jesus' name, amen.

> "[God] is able to do exceedingly
> abundantly above all that we
> ask or think" (Eph. 3:20).

Father,
You are good.

_____

_____

_____

_____

_____

_____

_____

I need help.

_____

_____

_____

_____

_____

_____

_____

They need help.

_____

_____

_____

_____

_____

_____

_____

_____

Thank you.

_____

_____

_____

_____

_____

_____

_____

_____

In Jesus' name, amen.

> *Nothing pleases Jesus as much*
> *as being audaciously trusted.*

Father,
You are good.

_____

_____

_____

_____

_____

_____

_____

I need help.

_____

_____

_____

_____

_____

_____

_____

They need help.

_____

_____

_____

_____

_____

_____

_____

_____

Thank you.

_____

_____

_____

_____

_____

_____

_____

_____

In Jesus' name, amen.

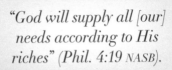

"God will supply all [our] needs according to His riches" (Phil. 4:19 NASB).

Father,

You are good.

_____

_____

_____

_____

_____

_____

_____

I need help.

_____

_____

_____

_____

_____

_____

_____

_____

They need help.

_____

_____

_____

_____

_____

_____

_____

_____

Thank you.

_____

_____

_____

_____

_____

_____

_____

_____

In Jesus' name, amen.

> *You are never more like Jesus than when you pray for others.*

Father,
You are good.

_____

_____

_____

_____

_____

_____

_____

_____

I need help.

_____

_____

_____

_____

_____

_____

_____

_____

They need help.

_____

_____

_____

_____

_____

_____

_____

_____

_____

Thank you.

_____

_____

_____

_____

_____

_____

_____

_____

In Jesus' name, amen.

> *"Truly, truly, I say to you, if you ask the Father for anything in My name, He will give it to you"* (John 16:23 NASB).

Father,

You are good.

_____

_____

_____

_____

_____

_____

_____

I need help.

_____

_____

_____

_____

_____

_____

_____

They need help.

_____
_____
_____
_____
_____
_____
_____
_____
_____

Thank you.

_____
_____
_____
_____
_____
_____
_____
_____
_____

In Jesus' name, amen.

> *Prayer is not a magical formula or a mystical chant. It is the yes to God's invitation to invoke his name.*

Father,
You are good.

_____

_____

_____

_____

_____

_____

_____

I need help.

_____

_____

_____

_____

_____

_____

_____

They need help.

_____

_____

_____

_____

_____

_____

_____

_____

Thank you.

_____

_____

_____

_____

_____

_____

_____

_____

In Jesus' name, amen.

Since God works, prayer works.
Since God is good, prayer is good.
Since you matter to God, your
prayers matter in heaven.

Father,
You are good.

I need help.

They need help.

_____

_____

_____

_____

_____

_____

_____

_____

Thank you.

_____

_____

_____

_____

_____

_____

_____

_____

In Jesus' name, amen.

> *You're never without hope, because you're never without prayer.*

Father,
You are good.

_____

_____

_____

_____

_____

_____

_____

I need help.

_____

_____

_____

_____

_____

_____

_____

They need help.

_____

_____

_____

_____

_____

_____

_____

_____

Thank you.

_____

_____

_____

_____

_____

_____

_____

_____

In Jesus' name, amen.

> *Prayer is simply a heartfelt conversation between God and his child.*

Father,

You are good.

_____

_____

_____

_____

_____

_____

_____

I need help.

_____

_____

_____

_____

_____

_____

_____

_____

They need help.

_____

_____

_____

_____

_____

_____

_____

_____

_____

_____

Thank you.

_____

_____

_____

_____

_____

_____

_____

_____

_____

In Jesus' name, amen.

*We speak. He listens. He speaks.
We listen. This is prayer in its
purest form. God changes his
people through such moments.*

Father,
You are good.

I need help.

They need help.

_____

_____

_____

_____

_____

_____

_____

_____

Thank you.

_____

_____

_____

_____

_____

_____

_____

_____

In Jesus' name, amen.

> *Prayer begins with an honest,*
> *heartfelt "Oh, Daddy."*

Father,
You are good.

_____

_____

_____

_____

_____

_____

_____

I need help.

_____

_____

_____

_____

_____

_____

_____

They need help.

_____

_____

_____

_____

_____

_____

_____

_____

Thank you.

_____

_____

_____

_____

_____

_____

_____

_____

In Jesus' name, amen.

*Jesus invites us to approach
God the way a child approaches
his or her daddy.*

Father,
You are good.

_____

_____

_____

_____

_____

_____

_____

I need help.

_____

_____

_____

_____

_____

_____

_____

They need help.

_____

_____

_____

_____

_____

_____

_____

_____

Thank you.

_____

_____

_____

_____

_____

_____

_____

_____

In Jesus' name, amen.

> *If God is at once Father and Creator, holy—unlike us—and high above us, then we at any point are only a prayer away from help.*

Father,
You are good.

_____

_____

_____

_____

_____

_____

_____

I need help.

_____

_____

_____

_____

_____

_____

_____

They need help.

Thank you.

In Jesus' name, amen.

Before you face the world,
face your Father.

Father,
You are good.

I need help.

They need help.

_____

_____

_____

_____

_____

_____

_____

_____

Thank you.

_____

_____

_____

_____

_____

_____

_____

_____

In Jesus' name, amen.

> *"Be anxious for nothing, but in everything by prayer and supplication, with thanksgiving, let your requests be made known to God"* (Phil. 4:6).

Father,
You are good.

I need help.

They need help.

_____

_____

_____

_____

_____

_____

_____

_____

_____

Thank you.

_____

_____

_____

_____

_____

_____

_____

_____

In Jesus' name, amen.

> *God keeps his word.*
> *We just need to ask.*

Father,
You are good.

_____

_____

_____

_____

_____

_____

_____

I need help.

_____

_____

_____

_____

_____

_____

_____

They need help.

_____

_____

_____

_____

_____

_____

_____

_____

Thank you.

_____

_____

_____

_____

_____

_____

_____

_____

In Jesus' name, amen.

> *"Cast all your anxiety on him because he cares for you"* (1 Peter 5:7 *NIV*).

Father,
You are good.

_____

_____

_____

_____

_____

_____

_____

I need help.

_____

_____

_____

_____

_____

_____

_____

_____

They need help.

_____

_____

_____

_____

_____

_____

_____

_____

Thank you.

_____

_____

_____

_____

_____

_____

_____

_____

In Jesus' name, amen.

Jesus never refused an
intercessory request. Ever!

Father,
You are good.

I need help.

They need help.

_____

_____

_____

_____

_____

_____

_____

_____

Thank you.

_____

_____

_____

_____

_____

_____

_____

_____

In Jesus' name, amen.

> *"[God] is able to do exceedingly abundantly above all that we ask or think" (Eph. 3:20).*

Father,
You are good.

_____

_____

_____

_____

_____

_____

_____

_____

I need help.

_____

_____

_____

_____

_____

_____

_____

They need help.

_____

_____

_____

_____

_____

_____

_____

_____

Thank you.

_____

_____

_____

_____

_____

_____

_____

In Jesus' name, amen.

> *Nothing pleases Jesus as much*
> *as being audaciously trusted.*

Father,

You are good.

_____

_____

_____

_____

_____

_____

_____

I need help.

_____

_____

_____

_____

_____

_____

_____

They need help.

Thank you.

In Jesus' name, amen.

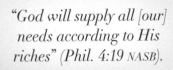

*"God will supply all [our]
needs according to His
riches" (Phil. 4:19 NASB).*

Father,
You are good.

_____

_____

_____

_____

_____

_____

_____

_____

I need help.

_____

_____

_____

_____

_____

_____

_____

_____

They need help.

_____

_____

_____

_____

_____

_____

_____

_____

Thank you.

_____

_____

_____

_____

_____

_____

_____

_____

In Jesus' name, amen.

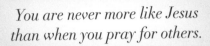

*You are never more like Jesus
than when you pray for others.*

Father,
You are good.

_____

_____

_____

_____

_____

_____

_____

I need help.

_____

_____

_____

_____

_____

_____

_____

They need help.

_____

_____

_____

_____

_____

_____

_____

_____

Thank you.

_____

_____

_____

_____

_____

_____

_____

_____

In Jesus' name, amen.

> *"Truly, truly, I say to you, if you ask the Father for anything in My name, He will give it to you"* (John 16:23 NASB).

Father,

You are good.

_____

_____

_____

_____

_____

_____

_____

I need help.

_____

_____

_____

_____

_____

_____

_____

They need help.

_____

_____

_____

_____

_____

_____

_____

_____

Thank you.

_____

_____

_____

_____

_____

_____

_____

_____

In Jesus' name, amen.

> *Prayer is not a magical formula or a mystical chant. It is the yes to God's invitation to invoke his name.*

Father,

You are good.

_____

_____

_____

_____

_____

_____

_____

I need help.

_____

_____

_____

_____

_____

_____

_____

_____

They need help.

_____

_____

_____

_____

_____

_____

_____

_____

Thank you.

_____

_____

_____

_____

_____

_____

_____

_____

In Jesus' name, amen.

> *Since God works, prayer works.*
> *Since God is good, prayer is good.*
> *Since you matter to God, your*
> *prayers matter in heaven.*

Father,
You are good.

_____

_____

_____

_____

_____

_____

_____

I need help.

_____

_____

_____

_____

_____

_____

_____

They need help.

_____

_____

_____

_____

_____

_____

_____

_____

_____

Thank you.

_____

_____

_____

_____

_____

_____

_____

_____

In Jesus' name, amen.

> *You're never without hope, because*
> *you're never without prayer.*

Father,

You are good.

_____

_____

_____

_____

_____

_____

_____

I need help.

_____

_____

_____

_____

_____

_____

_____

They need help.

_____

_____

_____

_____

_____

_____

_____

_____

_____

Thank you.

_____

_____

_____

_____

_____

_____

_____

_____

In Jesus' name, amen.